TAVISTO

NORTH & SOUTH

by A.R. Kingdom

ARK PUBLICATIONS
(RAILWAYS)

First published in 2006 by ARK PUBLICATIONS (RAILWAYS), an imprint of
FOREST PUBLISHING, Woodstock, Liverton, Newton Abbot, Devon TQ12 6JJ

British Library Cataloguing in Publication Data
A catalogue record for this book is available from the British Library
ISBN 1–873029–12–8

Tavistock South Station on 22nd December 1962, showing 2-6-2T No. 5569 about
to depart for Launceston on the 10.40 a.m. service from Plymouth.

Peter W. Gray

ARK PUBLICATIONS (RAILWAYS)
Editorial, layout and design by:
Mike Lang

Typeset by:
Carnaby Typesetting, Torquay, Devon TQ1 1EG

Printed and bound in Great Britain by:
Wotton Printers Limited, Newton Abbot, Devon TQ12 4PJ

Cover photographs:

Front – Tavistock North Station viewed from the west, with a diesel multiple unit
waiting at the 'down' platform before continuing its journey to Plymouth
in May 1968.

Bernard Mills

Back – A fine view of Tavistock South Station looking eastwards. The locomotive
alongside the 'up' platform is 0-6-0PT No. 6430, which is about to depart
for Plymouth with an empty stock working at 2.0 p.m. on 23rd June 1962.

Peter W. Gray

CONTENTS

Page

Introduction 3
Tavistock North – A general description 5
Tavistock North – A pictorial survey 9
Tavistock South – A general description 26
Tavistock South – A pictorial survey 30
Bibliography 48

ACKNOWLEDGEMENTS

All photographs are by the late F. J. T. Elliott of Tavistock, except where they are individually acknowledged.

Bryan Gibson (photograph captions); Kodak Express; Steve Fryer; Mike Lang.

INTRODUCTION

Nowadays it is difficult to imagine that from the latter years of the 19th century up until the 1960s the important stannary and market town of Tavistock had not one, but two railway stations. Of these, the first to be opened (in 1859) was situated on what is now the site of the fire and ambulance stations and was originally the terminus of the South Devon & Tavistock Railway Company's branch line from Plymouth: this was before the route was extended to Launceston in 1865 and Tavistock became a through station. Later, in 1890, a second station was officially opened close to where now stand the council offices and some private housing. The reason for it was that Tavistock was included in the main line route from Waterloo to Plymouth when the last section from Lydford Junction to Plymouth was opened as the Plymouth, Devonport & South West Junction Railway. This was operated firstly by the London & South Western Railway Company and later by the Southern Railway Company until nationalisation in 1948; the line then came under the control of British Railways (Southern Region) and, finally, the Western Region.

My first memorable encounter with Tavistock North was during a bright, sunny but cold afternoon on 16th January 1954. On that occasion my wife and I were travelling on the 4.0 p.m. train to Waterloo from Plymouth, and this was one of its stopping points.

As the steam swirled up around the windows from the carriage heating, the door to our compartment was suddenly opened by a large and widely smiling ticket collector. Then, as I reached into my pocket for our tickets, he exclaimed that his congratulations were in order and he wished us a long and happy life together.

We both looked surprised as we had already carefully divested ourselves of every speck of confetti in the toilets of adjacent carriages! Anyway, I said "Thank you very much, surely it's not that obvious?"

"Obviously you haven't seen the outside of the carriage", he replied. "There is written in bright red lipstick under your window 'Just Married' in foot high letters". He then went on, "I think you both had better come with me if you don't want to be stared and waved at at every stop, I'll find you a nice quiet 1st class compartment of your own." This he did, and after we were settled in it he drew down the blinds on the corridor side and promised to let us know when we were approaching Templecombe. (That was where we had to change to the Somerset & Dorset for Bournemouth West to reach our honeymoon destination.) Just imagine that happening today!

My first recollections of Tavistock South, however, are much earlier. They include the evacuation of my sister and her baby son from Plymouth following the Blitz; later wartime trips with my mother and aunt as afternoon 'outings'; and weekly journeys to Launceston for the Post Office Engineers, when, over a long period of time during 1952/53, we installed new rural telephone exchanges at St Genneys, Boscastle and Tintagel, in Cornwall. (We used to leave our van at Launceston Postal Garage for the duration of these jobs.)

Over the years that followed I became well acquainted with both stations because of my work. During the late spring and summer of 1955 Seimens Contractors were installing the new STD automatic exchange in Pixon Lane. I was the testing officer and often, if the clerk of works was absent for any reason, I could, by leaving early, just make the 5.38 p.m. stopping train from Lydford to Plymouth at Tavistock North instead of going through my normal routine of catching the branch line train at 6.35 p.m. from the GWR station. However, this meant a terrifying sprint out of the exchange, down Pixon Lane, across the Meadows, and through Bedford Square to a long and horrifying flight of steps rising up the steep Kilworthy Hill to the forecourt of the station. I often arrived in a state of collapse, probably finding the train was late! Nevertheless, on these occasions I could be home an hour earlier.

It was not until after my son, Roger, was born in 1960 that I visited Tavistock South again. It was during the last summer of operation in 1962 and it was my son's first ride on a train; he also made the journey again with his mother and I a few months later in the wintery December of its closure, but before the last trains were snowed in. Future trips, I fear, were by car and to watch the painful demise and destruction of the station in 1964.

Tavistock North survived another six years and we were all on the last passenger train passing through it.

Finally, I should explain that the purpose of this book, the fourth in the popular 'Railway ARKives' series, is to describe and compare these two important stations (both known simply as 'Tavistock' up until 1949) and to illustrate their main features and functions by means of a number of contemporary photographs, many never previously published. In so doing, I hope that I have given pleasure to those who used and loved either or both of these locations, and stimulated all those with an interest in our local railway heritage.

A.R. Kingdom

March 2006

TAVISTOCK NORTH

A general description

Trains on the main line from Plymouth to Exeter and Waterloo entered Tavistock North Station from a south-westerly direction via the Watts Road cutting and the 480-feet long, eight-arched Tavistock viaduct, which was crossed some 70 feet above the ground at its highest point. At the eastern end of the viaduct (also known locally as the Bannawell Street viaduct, and almost 30 feet wide) the 'up' and 'down' main lines were furnished with a crossover, roughly at a point directly above Drake Road. A clear passage through the station itself followed with no complications in the track layout. However, at the eastern end of the station confines it became somewhat complex, for here, between the ends of the two platforms, was the commencement of a second crossover connecting the 'up' and 'down' main lines. Furthermore, on the 'up' side there was also a 'double slip' to provide access to the goods yard, which was situated on the northern side of the station site, whilst on the 'down' line there was a trailing connection leading to a headshunt and a reverse carriage siding that ran alongside the premises of a builders' merchant to the south.

The track layout within the goods yard was even more complex and featured two lengthy sidings serving the goods handling area and extending to the eastern extremity of the station site. They, too, were interconnected with two crossovers, whilst further pointwork provided for four reverse sidings to run in a westerly direction. Of these, one passed through the goods shed, another served cattle pens and some business premises situated at the northern extremity of the station site, and the remaining two, both comparatively short, terminated in stop blocks situated adjacent to, and to the rear of, the signal box, at the eastern end of the 'up' platform.

Moving on from the track layout, the station itself was an elegant affair built to PD & SWJR design and predominantly of moorland granite extracted from the contractor's own quarries near Princetown. This quarried stone, being of irregular shape and size, meant that the walls of the main station buildings had a 'crazy paving' pattern, which was accentuated by the use of a dark mortar. In addition, some of the granite was faced with blue bricks employed as edging around the windows and doorways, and also as finishing to each corner, so the overall effect was extremely attractive. The blue bricks, incidentally, were manufactured in nearby Gunnislake, in east Cornwall, so were not the ubiquitous 'Staffordshire Blues' seen in most other stations.

As was standard practice on the PD & SWJR, the main station buildings were situated on the 'down' side. Besides incorporating the stationmaster's house, these accommodated booking and parcels offices, general and ladies' waiting rooms, and a refreshment room. There was also a large waiting room on the 'up' platform, which was constructed in matching style.

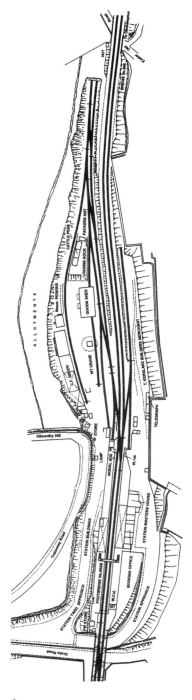

Courtesy and copyright Irwell Press Limited, from *The Okehampton Line* by John Nicholas and George Reeve, published by Irwell Press 2001.

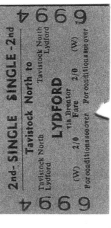

The 'up' and 'down' platforms were 350-feet and 375-feet long respectively and, again, were built of local stone. Both were surfaced with tarmac – it is believed that Tavistock North was one of the first stations to have had its platforms surfaced in this manner – and they were edged with blue bricks, for many years painted white for safety reasons. Both platforms were also partly protected from the elements by canopies attached, on the lineside, to the main station buildings and the waiting room. These were supported on locally manufactured, ornate, cast-iron columns with large and equally ornate Victorian brackets, six of them spaced at regular intervals for the 'down' side canopy and five for the shorter one on the 'up' side. The canopies themselves were constructed of vertical wooden planking with rounded lower ends and had pitched roofs made up of a slate covering on the lineside and a glass-panelled covering on the other.

Public access between the platforms was provided in the form of an attractive lattice-sided iron footbridge with a corrugated iron roof. This was situated just beyond the western ends of the two canopies and was built by Arroll Brothers of Glasgow, famous for the construction of the Forth Bridge. (At the time of writing the footbridge resides at the Plym Valley Railway site at Marsh Mills in a semi-derelict state and is awaiting restoration.)

Lighting on the platforms was originally provided by gas lamps, mounted on cast-iron pillars; they were fed by gas produced at the local gasworks. However, when the station was converted to electric lighting in the 1950s the electric lamps that replaced them were mounted on far less elegant concrete posts, which were manufactured at Exmouth Junction but not at all in keeping with the station. The same was true as regards the four station nameboards when they, too, were repositioned on matching concrete posts.

Both platforms were also equipped with water cranes. One stood on the 'down' side at the western end, close to a wooden foot crossing for station staff, and the other was on the 'up' side at the eastern end, in close proximity to the signal box. This, in turn, was constructed to PD & SWJR design, like the main station buildings, and consisted of a wide, brick base, timber-framed top and a hipped roof of grey slate. It also had a porch constructed of vertical wooden planking and a flight of wooden steps on its western elevation in order to provide a means of access, and was fitted out with a Stevens, 21-lever frame which controlled the requisite signals for the day-to-day running of the station.

The main signalling for Tavistock North followed a familiar pattern for a station of its size. On the Plymouth side the 'up distant' and 'up home' signals were situated at 1,151 yards and 314 yards respectively from the centre of the signal box, whilst the 'down starter' and 'down advanced starter' stood 151 yards and 328 yards away respectively, the former situated at the end of the 'down' platform. Similarly, on the Brentor side, the 'down distant' and 'down home' signals were situated at 1,157 yards and 74 yards respectively from the centre of the signal box, whilst the 'up advanced starter' stood 389 yards away. However, the 'up starter' was situated just outside the signal box and was a feature of the station's signalling system as it was fitted on a tall, lattice-patterned signal post which also had a 'double signal' mounted on it at a much higher level. The reason for this was that the lower signal arm was difficult for train drivers to see as they approached the station from the Plymouth direction because of the footbridge being in their line of sight.

Turning now to the station site as a whole, it was situated high up on the northern fringe of Tavistock and overlooked both the town and the surrounding countryside. However, from the town centre it was quite difficult to reach because of the lengthy uphill climb involved, which commenced in Bedford Square (named after Francis Russell, the 7th Duke of Bedford, who remodelled the town during the 1840s). From Bedford Square, the climb continued into Drake Road and then, not long after passing under the second arch of the viaduct from its eastern end, into the road leading directly to the station (now Kilworthy Park and Quant Park). This, in turn, ran in the opposite direction to Drake Road, went past the station yard approach on the 'up' side of the station (on the left), under the first arch of the viaduct and, finally, led into the station approach and forecourt on the 'down' side. A lesser-used means of access to the station – for the fit and energetic – was the steep, stepped approach from Kilworthy Hill to a point on the forecourt opposite the main entrance.

Viewed from the forecourt, the outside appearance of the main station buildings was that of clean cut lines pleasing to the architectural eye, and, as previously stated, they were built predominantly of quarried moorland granite, which supported a long apexed slate roof. The front wall was punctuated with the main entrance doors, six pairs of windows (two under the entrance canopy) and one single window. These were all edged with blue bricks, and the windows were all sash windows, the top halves each having six small panes. In addition, three dormers protruded from the main roof, each having a six-paned window and matching slate roof. Two multi-chimney brick stacks gave venting to the waiting room fire and those in other offices. The whole facade was completed at its eastern end by the adjoining stationmaster's house, a matching building and two stories high; this had an apex roof at 90 degrees to the station and was equipped with two brick chimney stacks providing vents to the six original fireplaces in the house.

In concluding this chapter it is pleasing to say that the former stationmaster's house and main station buildings on the 'down' side are still intact; they are now privately owned and used daily even though not yet fully restored. Sadly, though, the 'up' side waiting room and all the other structures were demolished several years ago and the site redeveloped to make way for the council offices and some private housing. The main saving factor is the restoration and use as a cycleway/footpath of the limestone viaduct which remains one of the main features of the town. The view from it is, as it was from a passing train, panoramic of the town and the moors beyond, and it is a place to dwell on a fine day.

TAVISTOCK NORTH

A pictorial survey

Tavistock viaduct viewed from the north soon after construction. On the extreme left is the deviation of the road to Kilworthy, the original alignment of which was breached by the railway.

Author's collection

The main station building and stationmaster's house located on the 'down' side.

Author's collection

A view of the two platforms and footbridge looking eastwards.

Lens of Sutton

On 17th July 1961 the 7.04 p.m. Basingstoke to Plymouth Friary goods train, hauled by a 'Westcountry' class locomotive, became derailed - just moments after passing an 'up' passenger train! On the viaduct it damaged part of the track, but only on the 'down' side as can be seen in this view looking eastwards from the Glanville Road overbridge.

Two more photographs taken on 17th July 1961, showing:–

Above: The derailed goods train after it had come to rest in the deep cutting on the Bere Alston side of the Glanville Road overbridge.

Below: Another view of the viaduct looking eastwards and showing that the derailment also damaged the parapet of the viaduct. Fortunately, although breached, the wall still prevented any of the derailed wagons from falling on the houses below.

An Ivatt 2-6-2T, on the 'up' road, meets a Bulleid Light Pacific on the viaduct.

Author's collection

WR 2-6-2T No. 5515 at the Bere Alston end of the viaduct. Western locomotives were regularly seen on the main line between Tavistock and Plymouth in connection with keeping Western footplate crews familiar with the route in the event of diversions.

Author's collection

Brush type 4 (latterly known as a class 47) D1676, on a crew-training turn, heads eastwards through the station.

Bernard Mills

The viaduct and station viewed from the Glanville Road overbridge on 28th November 1965.

The view eastwards from the footbridge over the platform awnings after closure, but with the entire infrastructure still intact (June 1968).

The goods yard on the 'up' side, with the main road climbing away at 1 in 75 (June 1968).

Facing page: Three more views of the viaduct, showing a south-bound three-car suburban diesel multiple unit approaching the Glanville Road overbridge (top), a two-car suburban diesel multiple unit, also south-bound (centre) and a quieter moment, which reveals the repaired section of the parapet following the goods train derailment in 1961 (bottom).

The modern trappings of concrete sleepers and flat-bottom rail did not save the line (June 1968).

The 'down home' signal, with the station beyond (June 1968).

The 'down' side siding and a view of the eastern end of the station, which shows the 1 in 75 gradient eastwards starting right from the end of the platform (June 1968).

The cramped goods yard and clear evidence of the excavation work that was needed to provide level track (July 1968).

The signal box, showing also the impressive 'double slip' lead giving access to the cramped goods yard (July 1968).

Another view of the signal box, showing also the distinctive co-acting 'up starting' signal which was made necessary by the sighting problems caused by the station's footbridge and canopy (July 1968).

A close-up of the underside of one of the station canopies. The 'up' side canopy continues to serve a railway purpose as it was re-erected at the Launceston Steam Railway terminus (July 1968).

The deserted platforms which only four years previously saw several daily trains, seven days a week, travelling to and from London Waterloo (July 1968).

The deep cutting looking south-westwards from the Glanville Road overbridge (October 1969).

Contractors remove the fishplates on the 'down' road in preparation for lifting (7th December 1969).

Facing page:–

Top – Only the rusting rails betray the fact that this is *not* a quiet moment between trains (July 1968).

Centre – The viaduct, with the repaired parapet still evident (July 1968).

Bottom – The same view as in the previous photograph at a later date – October 1969 – with a symbolic shadow spreading over track in the early stages of vegetation. The shiny rails of the 'up' track is ominous evidence that demolition trains are in the area.

With the 'down' road rails taken out but not yet recovered, a wagon for the fishplates is parked on the 'up' road (9th December 1969).

A telephoto view into the station shows track-lifting at an advanced stage, but a short section temporarily surviving in the 'down' platform.

A pile of sleepers across the severed 'up' road marks the railhead on the viaduct.

Rails are loaded onto what will be the last train to be seen from Tavistock North Station (20th January 1970).

The redundant viaduct seen from Drake Road (16th March 1975).

The view of the junction with Drake Road, showing the approach roads to each side of the station (16th March 1975).

The derelict station seen in evening sunshine (January 1976).

The track bed towards Brentor as seen from the eastern end of the station (August 1970).

TAVISTOCK SOUTH

A general description

Although not situated on a main line like its more northern counterpart, Tavistock South was certainly not inferior as it was the busiest and considered the most important station on the whole of the Launceston branch. It also possessed by far the most complex and comprehensive track layout of the intermediate stations along the branch and, indeed, one that easily surpassed those at the vast majority of all other branch line stations.

A rebuild of the original Brunel design of the 1850s following a fire in 1887, Tavistock South was also ideally situated, being very near to the town centre; the station stood at only a slightly higher level and was just on the other (southern) side of the River Tavy. For a modeller, too, it was an ideal subject, as the total length of track within its confines exceeded 1½ miles and the station was so arranged as to contain all the various impedimenta needed to serve a busy moorland market town.

Trains travelling over the Launceston branch from Plymouth approached the station from a southerly direction on a right-hand curve, and would first encounter the 'down home' signal just prior to crossing the 25-feet span of the stone-built bridge over Pixon Lane. Then, as they crosssed the bridge, they would go over a set of points which connected the incoming single line to individual 'up' and 'down' platform lines. These, in turn, ran throughout the entire length of the station and continued almost as far as the bridge over Old Plymouth Road (at the northern extremity of the station site), where they converged and were connected to the incoming single line from the Lydford direction by another set of points.

In between the two platform lines there was also a third, slightly shorter, line known as 'Middle Siding'. This, too, ran throughout the entire length of the station and was connected to both the 'up' and 'down' platform lines at the southern and northern ends respectively. In addition, further pointwork towards the southern end of the middle siding provided a second means of access to the 'down' line as well as to a selection of sidings situated on the north-western side of the station site. These included two main sidings that ran towards the direction of Lydford and passed through the goods shed to stop blocks at the far end, and another that terminated in a gentle curve behind the goods shed; this third siding also ran back in a southerly direction to the timber stores, coal stores and weighbridge. Finally, a turntable road ran south-westwards from the 'down' line and yet another, short, siding ran north-eastwards from the 'up' line to serve cattle pens situated at the rear of the signal box. All the sidings, incidentally, were equipped with catch points to protect the running line from accidental entry.

Unlike Tavistock North, the main station building was situated on the 'up' side and was constructed of cut limestone with red brick surrounds on each window and doorway. This was enhanced by a fine cut Welsh slate

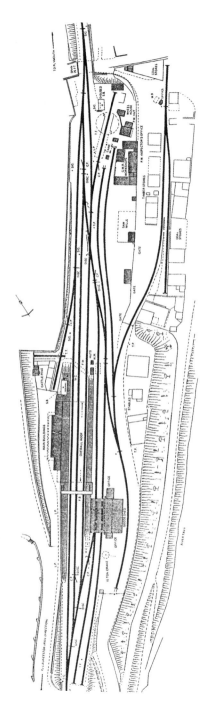

Reproduced courtesy of British Railways Board.

roof interspersed with several red brick chimney stacks of a square, 'chunky' design. The stacks were capped with one or a pair of buff chimney pots. Inside the building, there was all the usual accommodation found at a typical GWR branch line station – booking hall and general waiting room, parcels office and cloakroom etc. – and it was accessed by means of a private road in from Old Plymouth Road; the junction was soon after the latter had commenced its climb out of the town centre and passed under the bridge at the northern extremity of the station site. (Immediately beyond the junction, Old Plymouth Road continued climbing away towards Whitchurch on a steepening embankment which, initially, ran along the station's frontage and was covered in a copious array of rhododendrons. Pleasing to the eye, especially in the summertime when the rhododendrons were in flower, their height also produced the rather odd effect of dwarfing the station buildings.)

The main entrance doorways and windows on the roadside were completely protected by a long square canopy, whilst those on the platform side were under cover from a superb example of an overall roof, one of the last to remain intact. Although this made the windows rather dark on all but the brightest of days, it did at least ensure that passengers waiting in the wind and rain that often blasted off the surrounding moorland were provided with adequate shelter. Large additional fanlight roof panels, once fitted with glass, were provided along the entire centre section of the roof apex, but this tended to provide more light to the middle road rather than to the adjoining platforms.

The main trusses of the roof were supported, on the 'up' side, by wall-supported brackets and, on the 'down' side, by no less than fourteen timber uprights, rising from the platform foundation level. In addition, the entire roof was braced with longitudinal and traversing iron tie-bars, onto which numerous vertical drop-rods secured the spans with deft certainty against force nine gales. Finally, long lateral timber planking framed the wall between the roof supports on the 'down' side, every third section being fitted with a window.

Turning now to the platforms, both were brick faced with slab edging and had blue Staffordshire brick surfaces throughout their entirety. However, they immediately differed by the 'up' platform not only being wider, but also by being much longer. It was, in fact, 480-feet long, whereas the narrower 'down' platform was a somewhat more modest 320 feet in length. They were connected by an ornate footbridge to provide passenger access between them, and this came complete with the obligatory cast-iron sign requesting passengers to use it and not cross the lines. The footbridge itself was situated immediately to the north of the overall roof.

Lighting on the platforms, right up until closure, was by means of cast-iron, gas lamp standards, each equipped with an ornate, 'swan neck' bracket, from which hung a round fitting and 'on/off' chains operated by station staff using a hooked pole.

In common with Tavistock North, the station was also equipped with two water cranes, each with a fire devil tucked under its arm. One stood on the 'down' side near the goods shed, and the other was sited at the southern end of the 'up' platform, next to the signal box. This, in turn, was a typical GWR affair built mainly of timber under a conventional pitched roof covered with slate and finished with ridge tiles. The rear wall, however, was of red brick, as were its tall base, parts of the end elevations and tall chimney stack which protruded from near the north-eastern corner of the roof. All-round vision, apart from the rear, of course, was accomplished by multi-pannelled sliding windows that ran the whole length of the platform side and by further windows at either end; the latter were completed to the apex with lateral wooden planking. At the southern end there was a partly glaze-pannelled wooden door and a small wooden staircase, and at the front, below the sliding windows, was a standard GWR cast-iron nameplate.

Inside, the signal box was equipped with a 37-lever frame which controlled the requisite signals for the day-to-day running of the station, including those on the main running lines. On the Lydford side of the station these were quite straightforward and consisted of the 'up distant' and 'up home' signals, which were situated at 1,191 yards and 231 yards respectively from the centre of the signal box, and also the 'down starter' and 'down advanced starter', which stood 115 yards and 350 yards away respectively, the former situated just beyond the northern end of the 'down' platform. However, on the Plymouth side the 'up starter', which stood just beyond the signal box, at the foot of the platform ramp, was supplemented with 'up intermediate starter' and 'up advanced starter' signals, the latter equipped with a lower shunt arm. These stood at 153 yards and 250 yards respectively from the centre of the signal box and on either side of the pointwork connecting the southern end of the middle siding to the 'down' platform line. Finally, the 'down distant' and 'down home' signals were situated at 1,188 yards and 268 yards respectively from the centre of the signal box.

This now concludes the description of Tavistock South, although it should be borne in mind by the reader that over the years since it first opened in 1859 the station underwent many changes, not least its rebuild following the disastrous fire of 1887. However, to record these (as well as the changes that took place at Tavistock North over only a slightly shorter period of time) is well outside the scope of a book of this size, and it is for this reason that a list of publications has been included in the Bibliography as recommended further reading. Sadly, it just remains to be said that nothing is left of the station today and that the only evidence of a railway ever existing in the immediate vicinity is the bridge over Pixon Lane.

TAVISTOCK SOUTH

A pictorial survey

Auto-fitted 2-6-2T No. 5572 waits to work the 4.30 p.m. service to Plymouth, whilst No. 5569 takes on water before setting off with the Plymouth to Launceston train (8th August 1961).

Hugh Ballantyne

A sad view of the outside approach to the station during the last months of service before closure.

Lens of Sutton

A 45xx class locomotive, on what is probably the afternoon goods from Launceston, draws into the middle siding on what is obviously an extremely cold winter's day.

Author's collection

An auto train taking refuge in the middle siding.

Author's collection

The author's wife and son pose by the 4.30 p.m. train to Plymouth, he after experiencing his very first train ride on it earlier as the 2.10 p.m. from Plymouth (September 1962).

Author

The 5.40 p.m. Launceston to Plymouth train arrives at the station at 6.30 p.m., whilst the 5.25 p.m. waits on the 'down' line to form the 7.10 p.m. Tavistock to Plymouth (September 1962).

Author

The southern end of the station, showing one of the two original signal boxes and the water tower. The other original signal box stood at the northern end, but was demolished after the introduction of the replacement box.

The 'modern' signal box which replaced the two earlier boxes and was located at the southern end of the 'up' platform.

The 'modern' signal box, as seen from the 'down' platform.

The inspection pit and water column.

The roof of the station shed, as seen from the footbridge.

The northern end of the station, with the three lines converging to one for the route to Launceston.

A distant view of the station from the southern end.

Looking southwards from the end of the 'up' platform.

Looking northwards along the 'down' platform.

The footbridge stairs on the 'down' platform.

The 'up' platform and footbridge.

The turntable, which was not generally used in later years, but was useful to turn locomotives involved in snow clearance.

L. Crosier

The rear of the 'down' platform and part of the extensive goods yard which, on account of the cramped conditions at Tavistock North, contributed to its short-lived survival after the withdrawal of passenger services.

Trains on the middle siding and at the 'down' platform.

L. Crosier

An auto train on the middle siding. The afternoon train had an extended wait before returning to Plymouth.

L. Crosier

A 64xx class locomotive on a train in the 'down' platform.

L. Crosier

The passenger station, looking northwards.

L. Crosier

One of the cast-iron, gas lamp standards.

41

The cattle road behind the signal box.

Part of the goods yard behind the 'down' side of the passenger station.

The conical water tower at the northern end of the 'down' platform.

The rusting footbridge, looking across to the 'up' platform.

The passenger station razed to the ground, but with the rubble not yet cleared (c. March 1969).

The signal box awaits demolition (c. April 1969).

The 'up' side station building still largely intact, but with evidence of demolition under way (c. August 1968).

The same view as in the photograph above, but with just one remnant of wall remaining (c. April 1969).

The overbridge at the northern end of the station, showing Whitchurch Road which was subsequently straightened (c. July 1968).

The overbridge at the northern end of the station, looking towards the town, with the new straightened road (not yet in use) just visible on the left (c. August 1968).

The new road, almost completed, which would replace the dog-leg under the Old Plymouth Road overbridge (c. August 1968).

The removed overbridge at the northern end of the station, showing the Abbey Garage (long-since gone) (c. April 1969).

The station site as seen during the summer of 1989, by which time it had been taken over by the fire and ambulance stations, and light industry.

Author

✳ ✳ ✳ ✳ ✳

BIBLIOGRAPHY

Great Western Railway Journal, No. 17, Winter 1996 (Wild Swan Publications Ltd)

Great Western Stations, Vol. 2, R. H. Clark (Oxford Publishing Co., 1979)

The Building of the Plymouth, Devonport and South West Junction Railway, Stephen Fryer (Published privately, 1997)

The Okehampton Line, John Nicholas and George Reeve (Irwell Press Ltd, 2001)

The Plymouth Tavistock and Launceston Railway, Anthony R. Kingdom (ARK Publications, 1990)